T0345539

Sickle

POEMS

Ruth Lillegraven

TRANSLATED BY MAY-BRIT AKERHOLT

Seagull
BOOKS

LONDON NEW YORK CALCUTTA

Seagull Books, 2018

First published in Norwegian as *Sigd* by Ruth Lillegraven.

© Tiden Norsk Forlag, Oslo, 2016

First published in English by Seagull Books, 2018

English translation © May-Brit Akerholt, 2018

'Here I Will Be' and 'My Shadow' are translated by Kristine Hovda and May-Brit Akerholt

This translation has been published with the financial support of NORLA

ISBN 978 0 8574 2 611 6

British Library Cataloguing-in-Publication Data
A catalogue record for this book is available from the British Library

Typeset by Seagull Books, Calcutta, India
Printed and bound by Maple Press, York, Pennsylvania, USA

I often remember
the iron knob
on the porch door
at home on the croft in the forest:
The gentle grip of hands,
the yearning of soiled farmers' fists,
had worn it thin like
that of a bird's wing

Hans Børli, 'A Door Knob of Iron'
from *The Ice Bird* (1970)

To my father, Sverre Lillegraven

contents

PROLOGUE

All This Rock

it all fell
in the fjord

the sky
the light
the mountains

blue in blue
grey in grey
wet in wet

all into all

it all fell
into the fjord

the road
narrowcurved
and rockhewn

all
this rock that
once spawned
on the foreshore
in the church walls
in the potato field

where did it come
from

even the houses
are grey boulders

and the pipe-smoke
grey, grey, grey

but then there is
also the marsh grass
the rattlerustleleaves
and the sundayclouds

soon hither
soon thither

back and forth
back and forth

and below the ground
the seeds

small green fingers
stretching and
stretching

through the mould
through the mould

dark mothermould

towards the light
towards the light

PART ONE

The Moon

lie down to sleep, but
in the light from the hearth
I see the smoke rising into the vent
and out, and far up in the darkness there is
something so white and shiny, what do I see in
the skysight, I say, oh, that's the moon, Father says
lifts me on his arm, covers me with the blanket, carries
me out the living-room door and the entrance door and into
the tickling clear cold night, we turn by the large birch, Father
points up into the blueblack above and says, look, the moon, Endre
it has always been there and will always be there, isn't that good
yes, I say, and in the coming days I often ask after the moon, and
my father and I walk out on the steps, and sometimes we get
a glimpse of something behind fog and rain, sometimes we
see it like a sickle in the sky, but for much of the time
the moon is invisible, it must be hiding, my father
says, you know, the moon always does what
it wants, he says, and since then this has
always been my very first memory

Mother and Father

my mother
is meltingsun
and buttercup

my father
is oldspruce
and soareagle

swings sickle
and dries hay
sharpens scythe
and turns earth

this must you do
this must you be
he says

only this way
can rock and waves
and mounts and shore
still be ours

still be you and me

The Cones

I hide the cones
behind the hangingroots
in the ground, under the
flagstone above the brook
in the empty magpie nest

they can do it all

they can be it all

sheep and pigs
hens and roosters
fish and fowl

they can
hop and hobble
sing and speak
carry and
appease

they can be
sister and brother
father and mother

Silence

you talk too much, Endre
my father says to me the winter
I turn four, so then I stop talking and
then I stay silent, so silent, even if Mother
coaxes and Father threatens, even if Father puts
the fiddle under his chin, lifts the bow, plays roomdust
into gold, plays the way I want so much to play, week after
week and month after month I stay silent, while the moon waxes
and wanes, stay silent while the trees turn green and yellow and
white, stay silent until one day I sit by the hearth and eat, and
a mouse scurries in front of my feet and across the floor, *then*
I forget myself, look at the mouse, I say, my voice full of
rust and dust, then I don't stay silent any more, but
the silence sits inside me, lying there, lurking
in wait, as if it were another language

What My Mother Says

Endre is something special
I hear my mother tell her mother
one day, Knut and John, they're happy
and wild like small boys should be, she says,
but she doesn't know that I'm sitting on the step
outside, listening to every word, yes, Knut and John,
they're high and low and everywhere, bite and fight and
pull hair, are like small boys should be, she says, but Endre
he's so strange, keeps to himself, speaks to his cones, but still
Svein talks to him as if he were a grown-up, as he is the oldest
and is to inherit the farm, while Knut and John, who are rolling
about laughing and laughing, without a single worry in the world,
who are merry and full of joy will go into the world when the time
comes and try their luck, if only Endre could be more like them
she says, and I can't say anything but one day I am going to
show her, show that I too can do everything, I can
carry everything and be everything

Nine Wild Strawberries on One Straw

christmas eve morning
the floor is dusted and scrubbed
and the room is decorated with fern
then my mother comes running from the
moss hut next door, she is shouting about the
fire stove in there and the room full of flames and
Father, straight from the bench and onto the floor, he
says that we have to get out, he lifts little Ingeborg and John
from their nests where they lie and make breathing noises
she with her thumb in her mouth, her other hand in her hair, he
with one arm across his eyes, lifts them up, carries them out in
the creaking cold, soon I find myself standing in snow and ice
standing there without shoes or socks but I don't feel the cold
or the pain, I can only see the sparks like gilded snowflakes
against the red sky, and there are Mother and Signe and
Anna, Knut, John, Ingeborg, Anve and Torstein and
Kristoffer, nine kids, nine wild strawberries on
one straw, that's what Mother says, and
thank god that everyone got out, that
everyone is here, but in front of us
the red glow is growing

the red glow grows and grows, and I
shrink and shrink, my cheeks glow and glow
for our house is burning, the beds and the table
pots and pan and blankets, Father's fiddle and the
faces I have drawn on the barrels become a ring of fire
and the buckets go back and forth, everyone helps, every
one of us lifts and carries, but we need more water, we must
harness the horse, the roads are slippery, so swish, swish, and
all the way the song in me sings that we will make it, that
we will save our house and the other houses, those that are
right next to each other, but we are too late, and we are
too few, soon our house is ash and charcoal but over
at neighbour Oddmund only one gable is singed
so we move in with Oddmund and them
stay there christmas eve and
the whole long winter

The Rock, My Rock

the steep rock above
the summer pasture
stretching towards
the sky up there

I have never gone up there
neither has anyone I know
gone there

but my father remembers
a fellow from the top farm
he climbed up the crater
splitting the mountain
in two

up there he stood
looking out on the valley
the land and the world

then climbed down again
came away from it
still alive

they have always been
so spry, these people
from the top farm

but every time I see
this rock, I think that
one day I too will
climb it

one day I too will
stand up there, feel
the blood beat and
the breath heave

know that I did it

then I will have seen
what there is to see

then I can live here
without longing
to leave

Grandpa and the Boat

seventeen winters I have lived
and forty winters has my father lived
he has been a wind, in the barn and the
cowhouse, in and out, back and forth, up
before dawn, in bed before nightfall, yes he
has been a wind, through days and autumns and
springs, but this winter, at Oddmund's, he has got
arthritis, lies with his bony hands on the bedspread
and aches so our mother can hardly bear to be in there,
nor my siblings, but *I* am there, yes I sit there, and yes,
my father is bent and twisted, like an old, crooked bear but
he is still my father, strong and tough, and now he wants to tell
me about something he has never wanted to talk about before,
which I have only heard bits and pieces about from Mother, now
he wants to talk about Tore, *his* father, tell me about when the
tar-treated boat with Tore Grandpa and his brothers and with two
neighbours on board sailed across the sea to follow little brother
Torstein to his grave, Torstein who used to lie down there in
his basket, waving his hands, who was now lying in
his coffin, and everyone knows that the
smallest coffins are the heaviest
my father says

the boat floats in the wind
and the boat sways in the snow

then they must thaw the ground
then they must hack the earth and the
coffin is so small, and the body in the coffin
so small, and the wind bites and the snow and the
sleet bite their foreheads their cheeks and their hands
bite them while they dig, bite them while they mumble
their words, while they throw the earth over the
coffin and leave the place, my father says
and I listen

on the way home
they stop at the guest house
they eat, and they drink, cheers, yes
here's to, cheers, cheerios, they toast
and they drink, what else can they do
now that he lies in the ground

they eat and they drink and they toast

until they begin to thaw
until the hurt begins to drip
from clothes and from beards
onto the table, into their beer
and onto the floor and into
the ground under
the planks

but then, in the boat on the way home
no one knows later what happened and who
says what, but *something* happens and *someone*
says something, something intolerable, that
makes the grief swell in the boat, and
perhaps it is my father who says it
stiff-necked and stubborn, yes
that is how it must be

for my father, your grandpa
he *is* the grief, and the grief is
a sledgehammer it is impossible
to get away from

later the whole village searches

for three days and three nights
they search

then they find the boat

and in the boat they find
two of the men, killed

no sight of the others
not on the foreshore, not
in the sea and not anywhere
else either

the same summer, when
the sun is at its highest and
the water at its calmest
a new child comes into
our world

then we are three
Mother and me and
little brother Karl

for Mother doesn't dare
to call him Torstein

nor Father's name either

no, his name must be Karl

Karl, she whispers

and *Karl*, I whisper
for I have never seen
anything lovlier than
my brother Karl
your uncle

that autumn
the two missing men
are declared dead

then they *are* no more
not my father and
not the others

now the life
and the world
can keep going

several years later
after my mother got
married again, Sloop-Lars
is in the big town and goes
down to the german pier

the autumn sun is blazing
and the skyearth is good

then Sloop-Lars runs
into my father

Sloop-Lars
sees my father

and my father sees
Sloop-Lars

they just stand there
and look at each other

Sloop-Lars has lost
his tongue

my father doesn't
say anything either
just barely nods

how's Svein
my father says
in the end

how's my little boy

oh, Svein's dead
Sloop-Lars says

why, he can't say

it's not true
for I am alive

Sloop-Lars
regrets it at once
for my father's face
turns white and grey
and white again

Sloop-Lars is about to say
that it isn't true, what
he just said, but then
my father has left

Sloop-Lars is ashamed
so ashamed he wants to
jump into the sea

but finally he plucks up
courage, goes to my mother

sits there for a long time
before he gets the words
out

then it is my mother who
goes so white and so grey

Mother who doesn't say a word

you must go now, she finally says
you must go now, please

he goes, and since then no one
has seen my father, your grandfather

he, the first one who didn't stay here
he, who wasn't like those before him

not like me and you
who stay here and take care
of a man's duties

Here I Will Be

I was the first
I will be the last

I will be
the burning
and the running
the lifting and
the landing

burn off
and rebuild

reap and sow

swing sickle
and dry hay

sharpen scythe
and turn earth

yes, here I will be
and bide and bear

bear stones and
sticks and slaughter
Brother and Mother
and Father

23

never like Grandpa

no, never like him

but always like Father

I see it now, as if it
were a godly light

that the sickle
and the scythe

the earth
and the water
the sky and
the fire

all this will
be mine

all this will
be me

Father and Mankiller

have I told you
about the awful bear

have I told you about
the mankiller, Father says

he is still lying there in the bench

the bear has
twelve men's strength
and ten men's wisdom

all saints' day, he hibernates

midwinter he turns around
starts to suck on the other paw

annuntiatio marie, he emerges

before he dies
he grasps a treetrunk
with the death grip

if they shoot
and wound him
he sinks into a lake
latches on to the
bottom

bearbile is good
for all kinds of illness
beartooth soothes
toothache

but if
the bear gets the scent
of a woman who is with child
then he may tear the child from
the mother's womb, take it
to be his own

that's why pregnant
women are hidden away
if the bear comes
to the farm

but it also happens
that they are used as bait

it happens that the bear
himself is the prey

now and then
those who are troll-skilled
recreate themselves as animals

but the worst is when
wicked wood nymphs bewitch people
when man merges with bear

such a bear can only be broken
with bullets of family silver

under the pelt
you may find the buttons
from the vest of he who
was once a man

but the mankiller
the killer bear from 1858
he took sheep and cattle
yes, people as well

poor Helge Vallevik on his
way home from haymaking
came across four bear cubs
hit one of them by accident
then the she-bear loomed

Helge was bedridden
for half a year or so
but saved himself

worse with Jens in Gjelet
out picking nuts, happened
on the animal, soon died

then the great tremor spread itself
men with guns took off, but no luck

they lay booby traps in the bear path
but no luck

in autum
a few sheep
went missing

young Åslaug
Oddmund's sister
took to the woods
to search

but she herself
trod on the string
triggered the shot
and fell, was dead
when they came
to look for her

a little later
I myself shot
the mankiller

since then no one
has seen bear
here

The New House

the fire
is in the past

there is
a new house
to be built

timber to be felled
timber to be delimbed
timber to be planed

Father still lies there
bearlike, but lacks
the strength of
a bear

with my brothers there's
mostly knees-up and beer-up

the neighbours help
like all good neighbours
driving load upon load
but mainly I am alone
in the forest

I am there
before sunrise
I hew and prune

all that is sad
I hammer into
the timber

all that is easy
I chop into the tree

pants and shoes
get full of holes
taking in water
and snow

my feet's frozen blood
red and swollen claws

but my cheeks glow
for it is only me and
the work now

timber and saw
hammer and planer
and all that is to be built

we will have a house
we will have a home

my father
the bear-killer
is sick in bed

but I will show him

I will do man's duty

one day I ask Father
to come to the window

he gets up
hops and hobbles
stands on shakylegs
looks at the new abode

you're like me, he says
and nods his head, just
a tiny nod, that's all

but out in the yard
stands his grandpa and
behind him his father
and then his grandpa

they all nod this tiny nod

good boy, it says
this is why you are here

here where you shall stay

clear and build
reap and sow

until you one day
hand over the farm
to your son and his son
and his son after him

that's how it is
that's how it goes

this is our fate
this is our fortune

and you are
only a small leaf
on the large tree

Three Rounds in the House

christmas morning
my sisters walk
to the brook

they don't talk
only take a rock each

then they will learn

loose rock makes loiterer
solid rock makes legatee

christmas eve
they walk three rounds
in the living room, with
flatbreads on their heads

they must be silent now

so he can show himself
the man who will be
their sweetheart

this christmas eve
I do like they do

put flatbread
on my head

walk three rounds
in the living room

my mother puts down
a glass of water
a glass of beer
a glass of milk

I get blindfolded

if I fumble
my way to the beer
my marriage will be rich

milk gives prosperity too
but water augurs poverty

now drink, boy, Mother says
drink, so we will know

so I lift the glass
and drink

Spring Herring and Polar Bear

Uncle Karl
comes home from
fishing spring-herring
makes my father
glitter and gleam

Karl has been far up north
to icy wasteland

disembarked
in novaja semlja
to hunt reindeer

then the storm came

to his luck he got to shoot
a polar bear, had no matches
and had to eat raw bear, the
meat gave him strength and
the pelt warmth, until
the ship returned

imagine
you're alive, they said
and looked at him as if
he were jesus christ

yes imagine you're alive
I say, I look at him who
has been everywhere
has seen and done
everything

all I myself have done
is being here, and that
is all I will do for ever

yes, Karl says, oh yes,
I have been far away

but believe you me
a better place than here
you'll never find

and *you* are Endre
son of Svein

here it's you who
steer the stars above
and teeming life below
down to the ants
in the mould

Lilacs and Apple Blossoms

just afterwards
Karl gets typhoid fever

in bed for a forthnight

then he is gone
he who defeated
the polar bear

in his coffin we lay
lilacs and apple blossoms
row him to church

then Brother John gets the sickness

after three weeks he too is gone
the good, cheerful boy

we all grieve, Father most

then there are eight left
eight wild strawberries
on a straw

The Forest Fell

trees I should hew
and trees I have hewed

they have stood there
a hundred years

now I have
put them on the ground
so frost cracks, so resin bleeds
and needles glow, for John is gone
and Karl is gone, and Father lies there

no I am wet and warm and breathless

I sit myself down here
wary of winter, chary of rime

I listen to the rush and roar
and the thumping heart

then I hear a little tune
then another one
and another

they turn into
a chirping choir

and *then* I see them

see all the chickadees

small fluffy balls
as white as innocence
but with long lanyards
dipped in soot

there are four, fourteen, forty

they flutter and wave
so snow falls and scatters
so nimbly nimbly nimbly
from the pine crown

the snow falls so slowly
that it hardly falls

the snow falls so slowly
I can hardly see it rise and
fall back to heaven, settle
down on the moon

here the trees
are heavy and dark

here is my body

it breathes, pounds
and beats

so strong and so tough

and then this white
singing birdwave

chirp chirp chirp

and just as quickly
all quiet

these birds

as white as
all this time
that will come
and come and
never finish

Everyone Leaves

Mother
looks out over the fjord and
her bosom has shrivelled a little
for today Knut left with the steamboat
from the pier where the world comes and
goes, again and again, and now it's only Mother
Father and me left, and then the girls, Mother says
and I say nothing, but Anna is married and has moved
and Signe is married and has moved, it is only Mother and
Father and me now, Mother and Father and me and the imprint
from the others, nine wild strawberries we once were, nine small
berries on a straw, but now Brother John and the first little
Ingeborg lie in the earth, and Anve, Torstein, the other
Ingeborg and Kristoffer have left for america, have
gone to the land of success, yes, they have all
gone, and it is so quiet, so very quiet in
our house

Knut

Everywhere it was so quiet, especially after that thing with Uncle Karl and Brother John, and Father just lying there, and it was so you couldn't breathe, couldn't live, and we were many, and it was cramped, and Endre was to inherit the farm. And of course I could have found myself a house and a wife, but it seemed so small, everything. And there were so many who had left, they wrote home about the great country and the great sky, about the plains and the prairies and about everything they saw and everything they were going to see, about the houses they built and the new churches and schools, and I felt a yearning, it called me. My mother cried. Not you, too, she said, because several of my siblings had already gone. And Father had begun to sit up, even walk a bit. He was so strong, my father, the bear-killer. But now he didn't look at me, didn't speak to me, not until he took my hand today. Farewell, then, he said, and I thought I could see his mouth tremble. I stood there with his hand in mine and didn't know what to say. Finally I let go, and I took my hat and left. But they have Signe and Anna, I told myself, they have my sisters, good girls they are, too. And they have Endre.

The Courting Boat on the Boulder

the field-girls are in demand
propose to one of them and you'll
have to suffer fussing and nagging and
hassling, the courting boat often ends up on
the churchyard gate or over the grinding mill roof
or in a garden filled with dirt, I myself put the boat in
a boathouse, where it sits safely, I think, here it sits safely
while I propose to the fine girl Kari, but as soon as I'm outside
they sneak inside, twenty or thirty of them, they get a good hold
carry the boat up towards the great boulder, fewer and fewer they
become, until only four are left, four blokes who put my boat out
on the edge, sail raised and ready, the next day I climb up with
my father who finally mustered the strength of a bear and
got up, crooked and ravaged and awful he is, not happy
but he does what is expected, he lifts, carries and
walks all the way up to the top of the knoll to
take down the boat that is now sitting there
a laughing stock

I jump in
to take the sail down

then the boat rocks
the boat lies there
and rocks

I stand in the boat
I look at my father
and my father looks
at me

he who has
roots for hands
and a bog for a back
now he pulls the boat
towards him

I stand there
gasping for air

what did the girl say
he asks

oh, she said no
I say

it was for the best then
he says

after all, you'll have
your own farm

New Moon

eternal time
the old ones say
beneath the birch

like grass on the rack
like yarn on the spool
like the circle around
the moon, around and
around

for all that happens
has happened before

and all that happens
will happen again

in eternity
nothing can be changed

in eternity there is
no entrance and
no exit

and there is a time
for everything

a time to be born
a time to die

a time to sow
a time to reap

and if the wagtail skips
around the plough

if the cuckoo comes early
or the magpie nests high

then there will be prosperity
then the partridge will cry
good qore, well cut
good qore, well cut

all that is to prosper
must be done during waxing moon

you must sow the corn in the earth
at the new moon

and you must thresh
at the waxing moon

bull must not mate with cow
at the waning moon

but calf
born at the new moon
he will thrive

you get most wool
if you shear the sheep
at new moon

and if the forest
is felled at new moon
the sap grows stronger
and new forest grows
faster

grass and flowers
are hallowed

grass and flowers
are like gold

so never
wallow in the grass
or tear up flowers

this you should remember
this you should obey

Abelone among the Hollyhocks

Abelone stands among
the hollyhocks in the garden
and talks to my mother, stands
there so tall and thin, she isn't like
the other girls, not like my sisters, they
say, she always sits with her books, she is
going to be a teacher, they say, the first in
the village, they say she is sharper than all those
she went to school with, could've become a priest
like her father, yes, if she wasn't a girl, my mother
says, and now she stands there among the hollyhocks
she who can so much and knows so much, she may not
be beautiful, with her pointed face, but she has the
loveliest mien around her mouth, oh it's you, I say
and *that's* the first thing I say to her, yes, she
says, yes, it's me

Abelone

And that's all I'd said to him before he came home to our place to look at the books for the book club, the one my father started because the village library never got new books. There is only one chest, but with the most splendid books, treasures which Endre picked up, one by one, opening, closing, while he was looking at me, as if to ask me which book I thought he should take with him. When he had left, my father said that this young man, he smelt of myrrh and cow and moor and mould, surely he had never read a book before, not of his own free will, at least, no, it wasn't the books he came for, just wait and see, we'll soon have him running down the doors, courting, Father said and grinned. I didn't say anything, because I can't stand that he talks like that, and I didn't know what I thought of that fellow either. It was true that he had looked at the books as if they were strange animals, had held the book so clumsily under his arm when he left. After this I didn't think more about him, but now he stands there in the middle of the floor in his finest clothes, a handsome young man he is, walking towards me, and I, who don't like to dance, who have never been one of those who throws herself into anything, what would Father have said, now I'm flung onto the floor, twirled round and round, and I don't have to worry about making the right steps, because Endre holds me. Listen to the music, he says, you're a natural, he says and twirls me round until I am dizzy and I laugh and laugh.

Midsummer Night

no longer can I bear
neither fire nor bonfire
not after that time, now I
lie on a shelf at the foot of the
mountain, and far down there I see
the large bonfire by the fjord, and from
here it is just a dot, the mountains are still
white on top, otherwise everything is so green
and so blue, everything shines and shines, shines so
it is almost too much, but you're much too fine to lie
here with me, too fine to become a wife on our little strip
of land, I tell her, but then her eyes look sharply into mine
oh no, she says, I'm different from what they believe, and life
it's so short, so short a step here, a step there, and then it's
over, like the distance from your house and over to us down
there, that's how short it is and now I have found the one
I want to share my life with, yes, if he wants me, she
says, oh you're a fool of a girl, I say and put my
hands around her, swing her around until her
eyes are just black strips, and she laughs
and laughs, until she and I disappear
become a large glowing *us*

The Good Child

Abelone on
my arm in the
quiet evening
the day after
the wedding

so nice and quiet
that I hardly dare
to breathe

Abelone, I say
I can't believe that
you really wanted
to be mine

she is
silent for a while
then out it comes

I guess
you'd rather have
Kari out in the fjord
if you could choose
she says

and I say no, no
it's you and only you
I want, you must
believe me

I say it one more time

then I cannot say it any more

then I turn silent
and we lie there in total silence

until Abelone says
I would love to be a mother

and I would love to be a father
I say

you'll be a good father, she says
you'll be a good mother, I say
it'll be a good child
we say

a child who
will till the earth
play and learn, and
love us both

a child who
will always feel safe
when there's danger

a little Endre
or a little Abelone

and the Kari-mist lifts

it'll be so nice
she says

it'll be so nice
I say

it'll be so nice
we say

and the
bluebell sky itself
will I pull down to you
I whisper, and put it like
the finest shawl around
your shoulders

The Legacy

now the time has come, the
farm with all its worldly goods
a horse, five cows, ten sheep and
two pigs, barn and storehouse, cart
and sleigh, outfields and infields, are
transferred to me, now it's mine, the farm
now it's my duty, and I hew and hammer and
clear and construct and shelter and shield, I'm
on the meadows and the hills, in the forest and
among the blossoms and in the byre, I am there at
daydawn and eveningdusk, the new moon, the waning
moon, again and again, the corn must be yellow, but not
too yellow, ripe, but not too ripe, the hand and the corn
and the sickle harvest and reap, and beneath the birch
stands my father, his grandfather, and his father and
grandfather, they all stand there with their arms
crossed and nod their tiny nod, for I'm son of
Svein and he is what I shall be

On the Blue Ocean

it is
autumn in the forest

soon it will sleep
silent and black

but it still billows
and beats and bleeds

one morning there
is a veil of cobwebs
and forestfog between
all that has been and
all that is to come

all that will rot
and all that will grow

it glitters and glimmers
and just *is*

you should not be
alone far away in the forest
you could chance upon both
bear and forest spirits

nor should you walk there
just to walk

no, you should have a purpose
hewing, hunting, picking

I myself am looking for
a lost ewe

I walk and walk
while the forest pulls
its green, rustling
train behind it

until *I too* am
green and rustling
until the forest is me
and I am the forest

here there is neither
rainrustling nor
trollputtering

here there is only
sagasoughs and shadowsun
and straws as tall as
man himself

I walk and walk

and like the cones
open

so the forest opens
layer upon layer

until I come to a glade

where blue blossoms bloom
even in september

never before have I been at
this spot, never have I seen
these blossoms so blue and
so small

they become the loveliest
summerdayfjord

I look around and wade in

lie on my back
glance up at the sky

hazel branches as thin
as Father's veins

green leafage like
congealed clouds

tree crowns
like wagon wheels
round and round

then I begin
to swim away on
the blue ocean

The Child in Everything

and then Abelone is with child
she is with child in the golden morn
over the crag, in the ribbon after the ducks
out on the water, in the apple shining rustle-red
on the top of the old Torstein apple tree, in the hammer
I lift, in the corn I scatter and the potatoes I plant in the earth
for this time it's different, it is beginning to show under the skirt
and then there is this new expression in her face, a warm wind
has wiped this angular trait, Abelone is with child, and god is
good, a new child is about to be born, a new child who will lie
in its nest, thumb in mouth, hand hiding in hair, arm
across its eyes, a new, little leaf on the large tree
a child I can carry out into the night, its arms
around my neck, and forehead against my
chin, look at the moon, I shall tell him
look at the moon

PART TWO

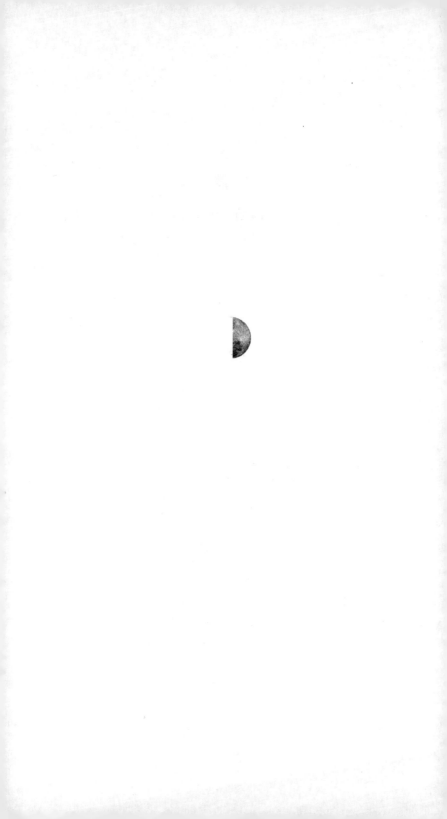

Silence Is a Cloud

the child
is in everything

and my father

he got himself up
with his bearstrength

like the corn rises
with the wind, the rushes
rise with the waves, and
the flowers with the rain

now he walks in front again
digs holes in the ground
with his crowbar

I go after him
I put in the racks, so
that we can dry the hay
so that we can make
everything right

if only
I had been able to
hold the racks

what's wrong with you
Father says

nothing, I say

something's wrong, Father says
that I can see

I am silent for a long time
everything shivers and drifts away

there's an animal in me, I say

it's on my hands
snarls and bites

and it hurts, and I get weak
weaker than the mother-potato
in autumn

now Father turns silent

silence becomes a cloud out on the field

then you'll hurt in other places too
he says at last

the devilry gets in your blood
the way devilry is wont to do

the bear lives in you
the way he lived in me

arthritis, we say here

rheumatism
the doctors say

same misery

in the olden days they
stuck a leech on you
or opened a vein
bled you

Brother Karl was so clever
with sick animals

people knew that

so if he was here
they'd send for him
at all times and from
every hamlet

for no one could
calm scared animals like him
no one could stop blood
like him, there was never
pus in wounds *he* nursed
he helped people too

sick and injured

I was the only one
he couldn't help

for against this there is no help

but remember, it only hurts
as much as you want it to

so take the saw, the rack
and the sickle

and do your duty

remember you can do it all
and you can be it all

At the Bottom of the Boat

I have always thought
that if Father dies, I die as well
but never that it should happen now
just after the end of field work, there
is nothing I can say, and nothing I can do
just have to sit here, not look at the coffin
or Mother who sits under her fringed shawl at
the front of the boat, not look at my sisters or
the fiddler or the rowers or Abelone with the child
in her stomach, just on the oars in the cold and clear
water, and know that I must pass on the moon, my moon
my father's moon, to my son and his son and his son
again, waxing and waning moon, in rings and
circles

Under the Winter Apple Tree

but then it happens this time too
afterwards Abelone lies there, silent
and pale and refuses to look at me, or
talk or eat or drink, just lies there so silent
and grey grey grey, and then there is all the
redness that I dug down under the winter apple
tree by the barn, women carrying a child mustn't
come near bear, but now the bear has moved inside
me, and perhaps that is why she's lost the child, the
next day when I tell Mother about it, she says that such
things happen, and Abelone is young and strong and will
have many children, probably as many as she had, so don't
think about this, yes, such things happen, and she herself
has lost a few, but a whole flock has lived and grown, and
she thanks her lord every day for that, like Abelone will
thank her lord one day as well, I nod and smile and
keep silent, but I know that Abelone will never be
like Mother, never will be mother, never will
get to thank her lord

The Fiddle and the Birdsong

Abelone just lies there
in the darkness and the grief is
a sledgehammer, but Eirik the fiddler
plays and he makes the pain disappear down
into the brew, down on the floor and down in the
earth under the timber till the water sparkles and the
moon twinkles in the room, till Knut and them over there
come home from america, climb up on the bench, sit with
a glass each and there come Father and John and Karl, they
smile and the fiddle sings like white chickadees in the forest, the
bear is not in me, and this is how I *want* to play, this is how
I *must* play, so at home I take out the fiddle after my father
I have the sky, the moon and the birdsong inside me, I have
Father, John and Knut, I lift the fiddle and the bow and first
there is whitebirdchirping and summerbirdrippling, but
then the bear is back, around me and inside me, he's
so angry, aims for my fingers and arms and shoulders
so I have to put the fiddle away, and so the darkness
comes, look, I tell the bear, I obey you, I do what
you want, I wont play any more, so calm down
but he won't listen, won't understand
doesn't care

Bear Dance

so one sunday
in red morning mist
another kind of bear
arrives in the village
down by the pier

russian, he is
but is led ashore
by two italian men

they have tied the rope
in a ring in his nose

oh, you, the large brownbear
what are you doing here

ah, you are dancing
and swinging around
standing on hind legs

everything they ask
you will do

and people
swarm and stare
holler and bellow

one after the other
crowd around the
foreign bear

Sjur from up-yard
Lars from out-yard and
Hans from middle-yard

they tackle it
break and bend

the bear stands there
towering, as if he can be
conquered, puts one after
the other on the ground

there they lie
they laugh and guffaw
don't know any better

they don't think
about the mankiller
they don't think about
sorcery and manbear

no, they mess about
frolic and gambol with
the bearbeast as if he
were a sheep

only I see
the sharpened teeth
the reddened eyes, only
I hear him growl and snarl
so hideously and huskily

you, Endre, they say
you've always been so strong
you'll be able to take the bear
yes, Endre, you take him

and yes, my father killed bear
my father killed the mankiller
and my uncle killed polarbears
and took the pelt for his own

but I just stand here

the bear has
thust his claws in my skin
and his teeth in my joints
gnaws and chews on hip
and elbow, shoulder
wrist and fingers

no one sees
and no one hears

here no one has
worked mansorcery
in bear

here no one has
worked bearsorcery
in man

here someone has
worked bearsorcery
in me

A Man's Duty

I try to take saw, stick and sickle
and do what's expected, be like *him*
but it doesn't work, nothing works, Abelone
has to do blooms and barn, and then the buds
come into leaf, and the land must be ploughed
and there's the fields to be manured, potatoes to
be planted, and fences to be put up, and cattle put
out to graze, and I, who have always loved this time
of year, I lie here behind the walls I myself have built
and shove the bear away while the sun rises and sinks
on the wall and I have been around land and shore, in
villages and grassy knolls, seen doctors and quacks, got
hot and cold packs and pills and beverages, none of it has
helped, and yes, you're a young man, says Doctor Kolltveit
but rheumatism is what you've got, you, just like your father
I saw you in your younger days, out early and late, out in
snow and wind, thinly clad and cold, you didn't spare
yourself, perhaps it was all too much, he says and
then he leaves, so I just lie here, do nothing
and am nothing

The Dream

so one night
I lie there, dream
and drowse, my father
comes to me

Endre, he says, I'd like
to have the deed of
the farm back

but Father, I say
surely you don't need it
where you are

no, he says, but I'm
thinking about Signe
your sister

you're not able to
get up again

you're like my father
you can't make it

therefore
you should
let go now, so
the farm doesn't
perish with you

this he says
then he disappears
then I wake up and
can't go back to sleep
I lay pondering

the next day I offer
Signe and Nils the farm

after a while
they buy it for an
agreed sum and the
vow of farm and grounds

so we get to stay here
Abelone and me

but I know that
I am no longer
like my father

so who
am I now

The Year 1877

what a dry summer we got
the hay didn't grow, now autumn
is here with hoar frost and no snow,
people fall on the ice, cripple themselves
and finally it snows, in february 1877, then it
snows and snows, upon metres of ground frost, the
snow drifts down for four weeks, day and night, march
comes and goes in the same way, the first of april there is
almost a metre, we've never seen so much snow here so close
to the sea, so there won't be any spring, no sowing until the
end of may, not until mid-june can the cattle leave their
winter pens, they walk around hungry in the garden
and we have to slaughter several of the best, we
have to empty the granaries, Nils has to go to
forestfields three days a week, and now
the bear has all its claws in me, my
feet are just lying here, and my
hands, everything withers
becomes thin and brittle
like the last autumn
foliage

Listen to My Heart

yes, Nils walks here

the way I walked here
and my father walked here

he looks after the animals
and the houses and the forest

does his duty

sows and reaps
sows and reaps

he does it all

but he doesn't do it
the way my father did

doesn't do it the way
my father taught me

but who can blame him
that it wasn't him who
saw the moon for the
first time on these
stairs

that it
wasn't him
who heard the
white choir chirp
one time only and
never again

that it wasn't him who
swam in the blue ocean
and dug the redness down
under the winter apple tree

that it's not his heart that is
ploughed into the earth and
carved in the timber here

My Shadow

the legs remember

the legs remember
how it is to be legs

and the hands remember

the hands remember
how it is to be hands

the blood remembers and
the breath remembers

everything will forever
remember

and like all things have
their shadow, like the books
and the specs and the cups
and the tubs have their
shadow

like the spinning wheel and
the stove and the benches
and the table have their
shadow

I too have
my shadow

I am
who you were
says the shadow

I am who you
should be

I am the son
of Svein

and you are
nothing

Abelone

The last weeks and months he has not said a word, and I think about what his mother has told me, about when Endre was little and didn't speak for a year. Not a word then, and not a word now, he just lies there and looks at me, and now and then he turns away. Talk to me Endre, I say, when I sit there. You know you can talk to me, surely it's better to talk, I say. Then I don't say any more, I say none of the things I could have said, I don't put my hand on him, because I know he doesn't want that. So now he lies there, and I sit here, and no one says anything, and I know they will study my face when I come out again, my mother-in-law and my sister-in-law and her husband. We are three in the farm cottage now, Endre and Ingrid Mother-in-law and me, and there are too many of us, I can feel that, although I do my best in the barn and in the fields and in the house, and I know they talk about him in the village, talk about him, who was once so proud and strong and full of arrogance, now he just lies there and cannot do a thing.

PART THREE

White Woods

then a book arrives
sent across the ocean
from Brother Knut

a book with
all the english words
and all the norwegian ones

a book so large and heavy that
I have to rest it against my knees

I push aside the bear
winterdull and somnolent

and then I speak again

what has Knut sent
me a book for, I say
to Abelone

doesn't he know
how I am now

doesn't he know
that I can't get myself
to england or america
or anywhere else, and
I have never read books
it's *you* who's always
reading

so what should *I* do
with this book
I say

but soon
I say the new words
as light as aspenleaves
inside myself

snow, I say
snow snow snow snow

and then I say it out loud

snow, I say
with my new voice
keep turning the pages
the sheets as thin as
morning mist

snow, white and cold
I then say

snowflakes
I say

trees, I say
the next day

trees and leaves
green and golden
water and waterfalls
waterfalls in the wood

white waterfalls in
the green wood

white birds
white waterfalls
and white woods

Abelone
puts her head in
my name is Endre
I say

snow snow snow
against my face
I say

The Cones Open

I am a leaf

a little leaf that
holds up the tree

like the tree holds up
the sky

like the tree holds up
and then lets go of
the cones

like the cones are at first
closed around themselves
but then open up

fold out their scales
let go of their seeds

and like the cones open
their palms towards the sky
and say: just come, all that
wants to come

come, all that
ought to come

come, sky

come as water
come as snow
come as wind
between my
fingers

the same way I say
come here, sky

let the cones open
and come to me

let the books open
open their pages and
come to me

let it all just come

let it all just happen

The Lost Bird

new days
and new books
come

have you heard
about the dodobird
I say to Abelone, she
is looking down into
her lap, doesn't
speak

have you heard
about the dodobird
I say again

now she looks at me
no, she says

I've read about it
I say, read about it
in the new book
from Knut

the dodobird
lived on mauritius
an island in the
indian ocean

it had a big beak

a big head
a beating heart
and small, useless
wings

couldn't fly at all
could hardly walk

the bird who must have
come to the island once
through the air

must have hovered
high above us

before it became so
big and lumpy and
unable to rise up

yes, it once had
a life of its own

and the forest with
its suites and salons
were its own

until people
came to the island
with pigs and apes
and rats

they were all stronger
than the bird

soon its forest was
destroyed

there was nowhere to hide

and the bird was unable
to fly away from there

two hundred years
have passed

two hundred years
since anyone has seen
the dodobird

Have You Heard

have you heard
about niagara falls
I say

have you heard
about the horned hog
I say

have you heard
about the phonograph
I say

have you heard about
the empress of india or
the potomac river, have
you heard about the battle
of wadi ras or giuseppe
garibaldi and his army

have you heard
have you heard
have you heard

no, she says
no, no and no
she says

how are you
really doing
she says

oh I feel fine, I say

now that I can look across

now that I can see
what there is to see

now that
I can see the world
as infinitely big as it is

now I can live here, I say

do you see, I say

then she rises
and leaves

Foreign Bird in the Fowlflock

just weeks later I sit
at the sunnywall reading
about a botanist at tahiti
I see Oddmund's family fowl
so fowly-powly-happy and
springrowdy reeling
and roosting
around

but what is this

a lead-coloured bird

with a beak as big
as if it were a ladle

a fowl it is *not*

I get up
walk closer

the fowlflock starts

but the lead-colour bird
sits there calmly

that is when I recognize it
from the drawings in the book

front-heavy, back-heavy
and slow to turn

dodo, I say

we thought you were gone

the dodobird looks at me
with needleeyes and dumbbeak
shakes its curved neck and
does a kind of jump
first once

then a second time

then it rises
flying fast upward

towards the sky
towards the sky

Snow and Sand

beneath the clouds
where everything
is so light and bright
there I potter around

down there is the house
where we live and breathe
don't know why

there is the sea and
the seabottom

see the sea
see the sea

and I read

there is the forest
with moss and moor
cackling and chirruping
with pine upon pine
spruce upon spruce
and birch upon
birch

from the steppes in the south
to the arctic sea in the north

we are the woods
it whispers

I read

through norway
finland and siberia

then I am over the desert

small sand grains
become clouds

descend in strips and streaks
snowdrifts and snowstorms

I read

and it is all
so fine and so smooth
between my fingers

oh the old brown world

until I arrive at
the jungle so green
so swelling and
surging

but oh
how dense it is
and oh how hot
it is

oh the old green world

I read

and in the middle of all this
a few white parts

they drop and descend

while it all spins
and spins and becomes
a round planet

oh the white world

oh the beautiful
new world

To Tahiti

since I am
a young botanist
strong in mind and
body, such a one who
endures everything

only inaction is
what I can't bear

like when my ship had
to lie at rest in rio

oh, so much
leaping and jumping
cabin-bouncing and bending
for the body must be kept in shape
and at night I jump in the sea and
I dive and swim in the bluegreen

I am Endre from norway

I can swim fast and
dive deep, come up again
with plants no one has seen
before

but then back again

into the sea
into the sea

hang in the main mast
look and look out into
this eternal leadgrey

until I finally see
the lagoon and the coal-sand
the palms and the mountain tops

ah, paradise, I say
paradise at 17 degrees south
and 149 degrees west

paradise, I say
even if the map says
port royal bay, king
george the third's
island

paradise, I say
see one of the natives
stretch out a green branch
towards me, a sign of
his goodwill

and I, wanting to
be like him, tear off
branch upon branch
pull them along
the beach

we find our own place
by the river, there we plant
the branches, sow peace in
the sand and call the place
port venus after the venus
passage we are here
to see

because soon venus will
show her true face, give us
the right distance between
the sun and the earth

I walk from cottage to cottage

soon I speak their language
soon I dress like them
sleep in their cottages

there's no finer place
than this, I say

as the only one on board
I learn the language
of the island

learn the word for dolphin
and coconut and shark

for nails, shoulders
and nipples

the words for *good, bad
bitter, sweet and hungry*
for *stealing, understanding
and eating, being tired
and being angry*

mahāna sun
marama moon
miti sea and
ra'i cloud

mata'i wind
fenua earth
ua rain

ahiahi evening
poipoi morning

tiare bloom
vahine woman

and *a hi'o, a hi'o*
see, see, look, look

topa, hōro'a, mau
to fall, to give, to hold

that way words open
that way languages open
that way cones open

then third of june arrives

I walk with king tarróa
and his sister to the
observatorium

through the telescope
I show them the small
black dot in front of
the big, yellow sun

look, I say, this was
what we came for

afterwards
I have to say goodbye
to the island and
the women

māuruuru for thank you
nana for farewell

for only mimosa
acacia and eucalypt
can come home with me

there they will grow, with
a view to mountain and fjord

see the new moon
and the waning moon

wind around the hollyhocks
and climb the birches

be left after me

The Years in the Face

she stands in them to her waist, the
white hollyhocks she takes care of year
after year, they grow both in height and
in width, while Abelone shrinks and crumbles
I can see her hair greying and losing its sunshine
all these years in her face, ten months of sun over
the mountain, two months without, again and again
while I sit here and lie here, read and read, while she
does all that she ought to do, but sometimes she just
stands there out in the garden in sunshine and shadow
looking at the roses, and I know that I should have
talked more to her, got her to tell me how *she* is
yes, I should have, but then I shrug, push the
thought aside, as if it were a little leaf on
the large tree a leaf that fell on my neck
on its way to the ground, *ua here vau*
ia oe, I love you, I whisper instead
but she doesn't hear, doesn't
understand

Abelone

I don't hear, don't understand. All these words, folding out from the book pages like larvae from the cocoons, take off and flutter around the room, more and more of them. It is hard to understand that he lies there totally silent one day, only to talk and talk the next. He, who has been high and low and everywhere, but who never wanted to open a book, now, after the dictionary arrived, all he wants is to bury himself in the books, now it is no longer possible for me to reach him, and I miss him, miss us. The books that were once mine, that I put away so I could be here, now they are his, and I miss them, too. I have hardly read anything in all these years, nothing but the Bible, and now *he* lies there and reads as if his life depended on it. And then there is this new language. Now and then he speaks Norwegian, but not about the usual things, not about things I usually talk about to Signe and Nils, about food and wood and heat and animals and clothes, and not about fiddle playing and the weather. No, the only things he talks about are the islands in distant oceans, seas and clouds, stars and galaxies, birds that have died out, and men on dangerous journeys. And I don't say anything, I just sit here and listen to him talking. Dodo, Tahiti, Uranus. Uranus.

Uranus and I

I set out
on a new journey
without education
or money, but with
a telescope I built
myself

seh den mond
Father said, carried
me out on the street
at home in hannover

seh den mond
seh die kometen
seh die sterne

and now I stand
here in bath

day after day
night after night

looking and looking
reading and reading

I *walk* and read
fall and land
on my back

get up, still with
the book in my hand
keep reading

I play, I compose
and I take students
teach them to play
the fiddle, for you
need something to
live on

astronomy, mathematics
and music are inseparable
woven together for eternity

everything is about
the art it is *to see*

see the moon, I say
see the mountains
see the woods

the earth is
the moon's satellite
not the reverse

the learned
don't like that

those who speak
right and write right

for who is *really*
this Endre

from norway
from hannover
from everywhere

they mumble and mumble
until I discover that a pole star
is not *one* star, but *two*

until I find uranus
behind jupiter and saturn

the seventh planet
the first new one in
one thousand years

two times as far away as saturn

now the solar system has doubled
the world and the sky changed

for cosmos is infinite

the sky with all its own
is always changing

everything
is created

again and again

and the way
a human life
follows another

that same way
new stars are born
where old ones
must surrender

Into the Sea

I hear
the fowl and the horse
the cattle and the sheep

I hear Nils
walking across the yard
back and forth
back and forth

now and then I hear
the friends from tahiti
and the science circle

they come to the door

hello, hallo, la ora na
is this Endre's place
they say

but Nils doesn't understand
neither Signe, nor Abelone
nor Mother

no, no, they say

and the bear holds me
so tight, so tight

by the time
I get to the door
they have all left

come back, I say

I am the conemother
I and the conefather

I can do all
I can be all

but no one is listening

I open the book
hello god, I say

let me free, let me
into the sea

let me into the cold blue sea

down to where seaweeds stretch
their arms and fingers upward
and upward, towards the light
towards the light

down in the waves
where the nakedslug
the ballan wrasse and
the sea anemone live

down to
the planets pore-animals

to the stars ray-animals
and the peacock-field
the bluegreen sun

down to the tiny waterflea
gold and silver combined
down to the moss-animal

snow snow snow
on the bottom of the fjord

yes, let me into the sea
ins meer, ins miti miti

until I am all and nothing

until I am *everywhere*
everywhere

Angry Abelone

she can't bear this any more, she says
she would rather set out, away from the
village and all the way to america, but she
can't do that, and she will be staying here, but
she will not come in here any longer, she will send
Signe or Mother in to me with food because this life is
so short, so short, just a small flash, that's all, and what
has become of her, of me, of everything, she says and what
day is it, tell me that, she says, and I don't know, what month
is it then, I don't know, I don't seem to know anything any more
it's spring now, she says, yes, I say, now it's spring, the cattle
is soon be put out to pasture, no it's summer now, Endre, she
says, and the cattle has been out for along time, that's
what you've become, how things have become she
says, dashes off and doesn't come back, I lift a
book, read a bit, put it down again, because
days and weeks have come and gone, and
the white bird chirping and the blue
summerdayfjord, all this that
was mine, what happened
to it all

All That Was

she who once
was lying on my arm

who herself was the water
and the earth and the sky
and all that was to come
and come and never end

she who shone of eternity

of the grass on the hayrack
the yarn on the spool and
the circle around the moon
round and round

while
the mountain was above us
and the fjord below us

while the mountains
fell in the fjord and
the fjord fell in
the mountains

that way
I fell in her and
she fell in me

that way everything
fell together to
peace and calm

that is how it was

that is how it should
always be

but I am lying here

and she
the one who was
lying on my arm

she too is
gone now

Abelone

There he is, and here I am. This is how it has to be, for I couldn't get him away from the foreign language or out of bed, and then everything sank and sank inside me. I have told the others that is just how it has to be, and they haven't asked, but they probably wonder. And Endre's books, they are lying on a table in the living room. He doesn't want them any longer, Signe said. Wasn't able to read now, he told her, and then he wouldn't say any more. Seven days have passed, and there isn't much left of this life, now that I can't see Endre any more, but I suppose it has to be like that, when we can't talk with each other any more, can't live in the same world. Now I lift up the book on top of the pile on the smooth, brown table, the book that arrived first, the dictionary from Knut. The book is so heavy, but now it opens, opens on a particular page, and then I see the word he has put a cross against. *Snow*, it says, with windworn letters. And *snow*, I whisper.

Egg in the Air

her voice is low and blurred
and I cannot ask one more time
however, I *think* I can hear her saying
my name is Abelone, yes it has to be, even
if it makes no sense, just a week has gone since
she stood here in the same place and never wanted
to come inside ever again, and she did not come either
not for seven whole days, and I haven't been able to read
a single word, but now she is actually standing there saying
my name is Abelone, then she becomes silent and I can see that
she's about to turn and leave, then it would be as if this had never
happened, so I clear my throat and say, *hello, Abelone* and that seems
to be enough, because she stops, and she says *summer, Endre, summer
and soon it's autumn, autumn autumn, the moon, Endre, the moon
the moon*, words she has learnt from the dictionary, perhaps I can
teach her a few more, she says, yes, I say after a while, *woman*
I then say, *woman*, she says, *man* I say and *man*, she says and
rain, I say and *rain* she says and *sun*, I say and *sun*, she says
and in that way the words fly among us like white eggs

Morning Glory

eggs, we say
birds, we say

fjords and fjells

sheep and sleep
hello and goodbye

good morning and
good night

five new words a day
that's what we have said

but sometimes it becomes
both five and six and ten

five and six and ten

today and tomorrow

that's the story
morning glory

sometimes there
is also a word in
german or tahitian

she throws them
back at me

and the days
are strangely light

as if they were
mother-of-pearl clouds

I get out of bed
pull two chairs to the window

opens it to the air and the light

then we sit down to look

outside the trees become yellow
and white and green and then
yellow again

again and again

the years hook themselves
into each other

the lines spread
across the face

Abelone, I say
one day

when
I am finally gone
going down into
the dark earth
I say

I don't want to go down
into a church vault and
certainly not under
an iron plate

no, I want to lie
in the free earth

beneath the open sky
where rain and snow can
water me, that's where
I want to be

till small green fingers
begin to stretch upward
towards the light

till the seed becomes
the finest, bluest
bloom blossom
tiara

PART FOUR

After All These Years

have not seen him for
three decades, not his eyes
and not his hands and not his mouth
neither have I heard his voice that sounds
just the same, he looks just the same, and it is
unbelievable that my brother Knut is sitting in the
red chair in my living room in my house in my country
talking to his crippled brother as if I were an ordinary man
as if I were climbing, hiking, trekking, he talks about his new
land in his old language, about enormous plains and heavenly skies
about people wondrous and well-dressed, but darkens when he
mentions his wife, she died much too early much too young,
they didn't have any children either, he says, anyway, *you* are
different, I don't know what it is, but you *are* different, he says
well, thank you for the books, I say, with an airy voice and he
smiles a reindeer smile and all, but still, *did you enjoy them,*
he says, yes, I say, *very much indeed*

Knut

Now they're chatting away in a kind of English, Endre and Abelone, because they have taught themselves. I myself speak Norwegian to them, because I hardly understand a single word of *their* English, but the two of them keep talking in this strangest of strange languages. I've been around the whole village since I arrived, and all that time Endre has been sitting in his chair looking like an old rotted tree. But to talk, that's something he knows how to do, he who was so silent and quiet, who always moseyed around in his own world, who was lying there in silence for years, they say. Poor Abelone, who was such a gracious person, mostly wandering around like a kind of decoration, now she has grown old, sun and wind and rain have carved her face. So even the refined Abelone became a working woman in the end, but she still has this strange kind of peace about her. It is with her as it is with everything here, all is different and all is the same.

Blue Rock

young Svein
son of Nils and Signe
takes over the farm
now

so it still stays
in the family

so we will stay here
long after my time

perhaps those out there
are nodding

I didn't become
my father

nor my grandpa either

I am who I am
and here I am

I sit in my chair
I close my eyes

what do you see
Abelone says

oh, I say
I see this rock
I never climbed

do you see it
do you see me

I am conemother
I am conefather

I can do it all
I can be it all

now I begin to climb
finger by finger, foot by
foot, and my body breathes
and beats and throbs, strong and
tough like then, it breathes and beats
until I stand there, look out on the
village, the land and the world
on all there is to see

then I rise and fly upward

towards the sky
towards the sky

The Ship Sails

sit with my crooked leg
on the stool, the window
open a crack

look at the ship with
Brother Knut on board
sailing out the fjord

such a
silvershimmering day
stardust in the fjord

but it blows, blows strongly

the ship sails
with wind and sun
across sea and cloud
becomes a swan, slim
and slender, but smaller
and smaller in the mist

soon it will
just be a little dot

the large ocean and
the large sky drift
together

soon the ship
will leave the fjord

larger fjords will
open and close
open and close

and then it will be out
on the large ocean, the ship
with Brother Knut on board

I sit still
my eyes turned
to the fjord

godspeed, I whisper

godspeed
and *farewell*

Abelone

Farewell, I think, as I stand there, by the open grave, in my
best clothes, with the fringed shawl from Ingrid around my
head. Down there is the coffin with Endre in it, soon it will
lie under the mound of earth, and around me are the crosses
and the iron plates with all the names and the large trees with
their naked branches, and I know so many here now, Mother
and Father and Endre's mother and father and our grand-
parents and many of our siblings, they all lie here, and now
Endre will lie here, down in the earth, in snow and in sleet
and in rain, until there is no more left of him. Yes, here he
will lie and feel no more pain, feel nothing any more, think
nothing any more, just lie here and not be any more, the
same way I myself will soon lie down in the earth and not be
anything any more. There is no rain, there is no snow, there
is no wind, everything is silent and black. I must go soon, we
must go home for the wake and everything that has to be
done. I will just stay here a bit longer, just a tiny bit longer. It
is still silent and black around me, but now I feel something
against my face, something prickly, and then I close my eyes
and lean my head back and I can feel it so clearly against my
eyelids and forehead and lips. *Snow*, I say. *Snow snow snow*, I
say. Again and again I say it. *Snow, snow snow.*

EPILOGUE

Up from the Earth

eternal time
like grass on the rack
like yarn on the spool
like the circle around
the moon, round and
round

for all that happens
has happened before

and all that happens
will happen again

all falls in the fjord

the sky
the light
the mountains

blue in blue
grey in grey
wet in wet
all into all

but all
this rock
that once
spawned

where is
it now

the houses
have colours

yellow white red
brown green blue

and under the earth
a new seed

through the mould
through the mould

towards the light
towards the light

Acknowledgements

The work with *Sickle* began when I read the diary of Ole T. Kjerland (1822–83), printed as part of Th. Haukenæs *Granvin's Saga. Second and Third Part* (1915). The story about the strong, healthy inheritor of an ancestral farm who became ill and had to sell his family's property, and who had no direct heirs, fascinated me immediately.

Being inspired by the stories in Ole T. Kjerland's diary doesn't mean that there is a one-to-one relationship between the diary and the poems. The diary is very level-headed and the style is sober. What I have attributed to Endre's emotional life in these poems, is of course down to me. And most of the poems in this book have nothing to do with Ole T. Kjerland.

I got the idea to the poem 'Grandpa and the Boat' from an event in Hardanger in the 1700s, which, among other things, is described in O. Olafsen's book *Ullensvang* (1907). One of my own ancestors was among those who went missing on the trip across the fjord.

The description of the popular belief is mainly taken from Ørnulf Hodne's *Norsk folketro* (Norwegian Popular

Belief) published by Cappelen Damm in 2008, and Halldor O. Opedal's series *Makter og menneske* (Powers and People).

The poems 'To Tahiti' and 'Uranus and I' are inspired by the two stories about the botanist Joseph Banks and the astronomer William Herschel in *The Age of Wonder* (2008).

The rest is mainly free imagination.

Thank you to friends and aides who have been reading along the way. They know who they are.

Thank you to Øyvind Rimbereid for thorough and skilful reading and useful suggestions.

This book would not have become what it is without the many long and valuable discussions with my editor Mattis Øybø at Tiden Norsk Forlag. Thank you, Mattis, for your eye, your thoughts and your patience.

The book is dedicated to my father, Sverre Lillegraven. Thank you for, throughout many years, nurturing my interest in the past and the people before us.

Ruth Lillegraven
Lommedalen, June 2016